Monday

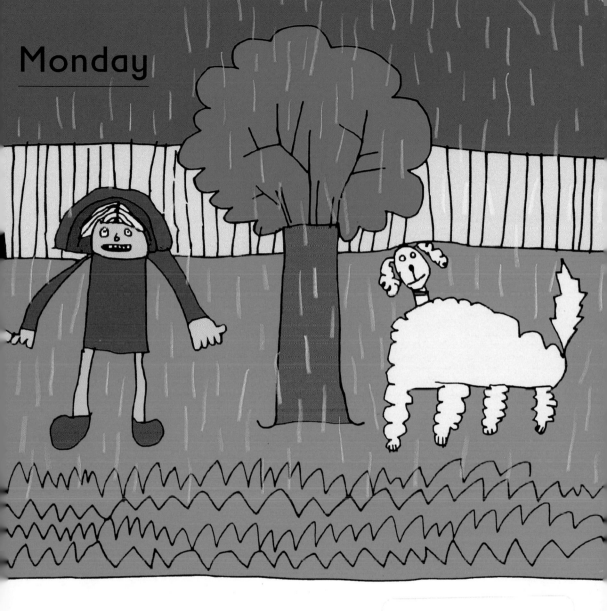

It was a wet day.

Tuesday

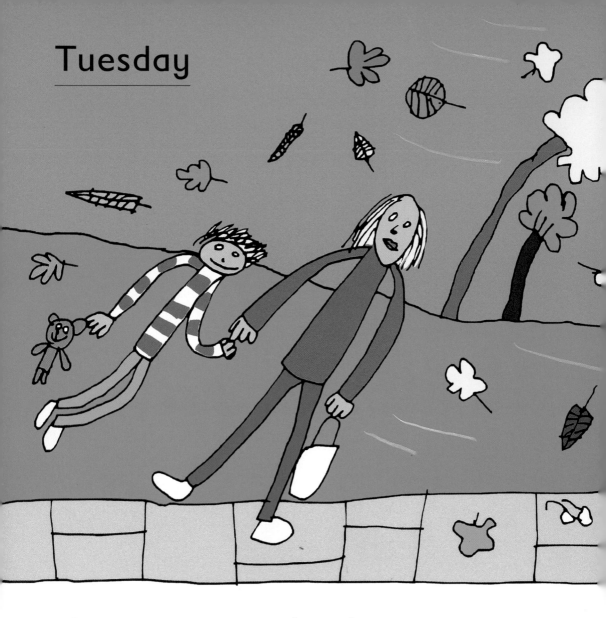

It was a windy day.

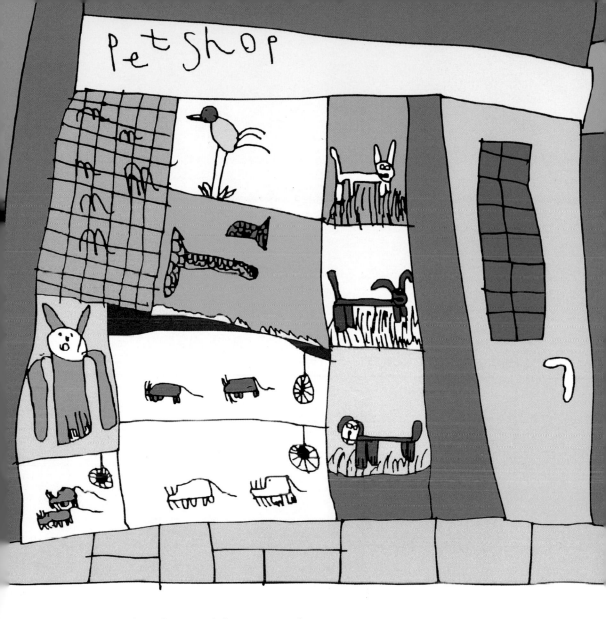

I went to the shops.

Wednesday

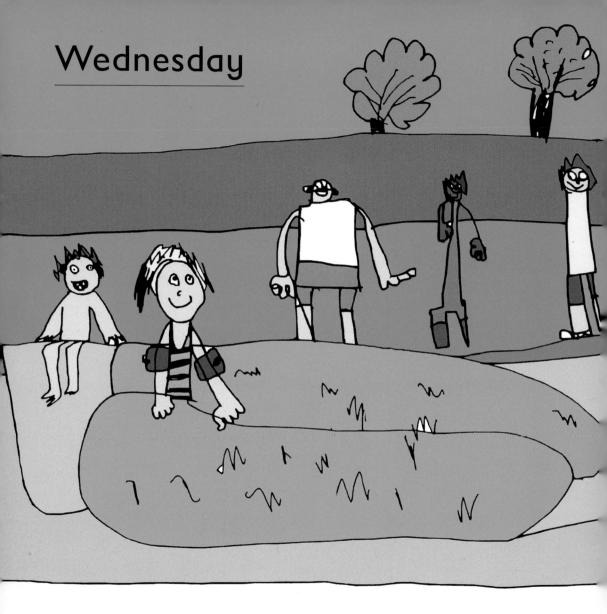

It was a sunny day.

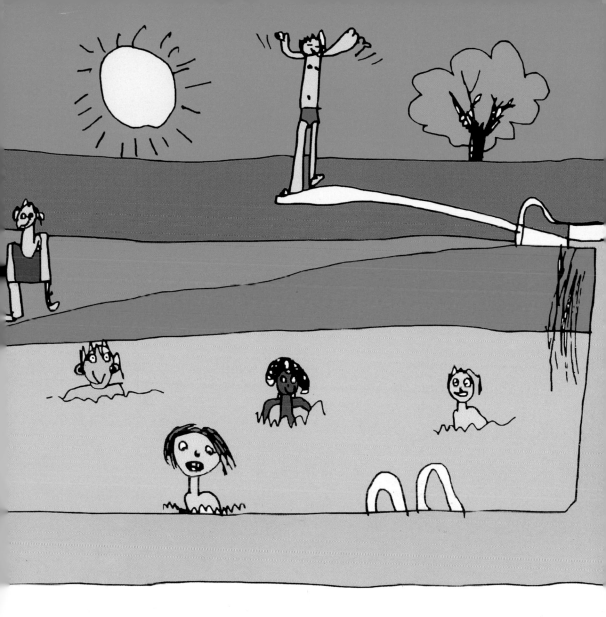

I went to the pool.

Thursday

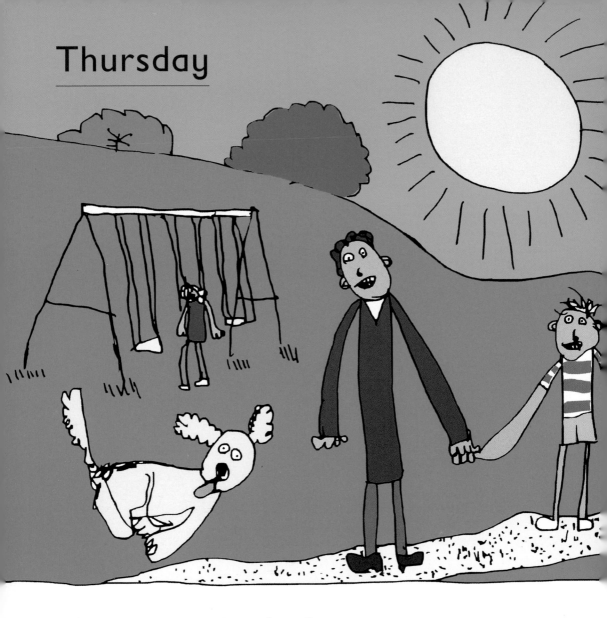

It was a hot day.

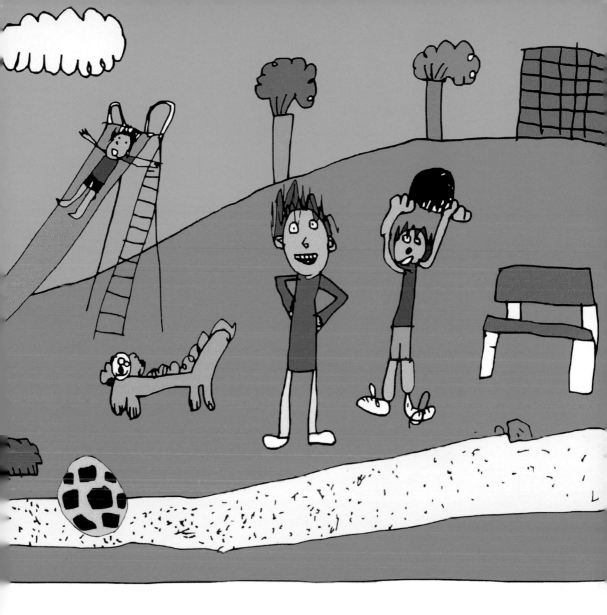

I went to the park.

Friday

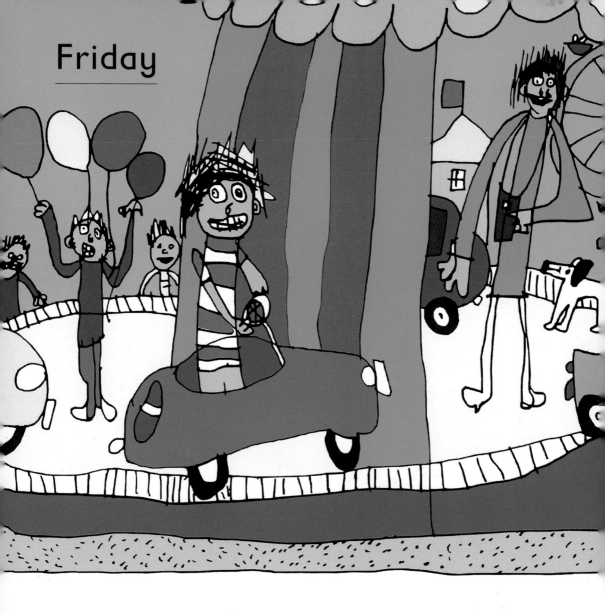

It was a fun day.